DATE DUE

APR 29 1995	

GAYLORD   PRINTED IN U.S.A.

BOOKS BY A. A. MILNE

Light Articles

THE DAY'S PLAY
THE HOLIDAY ROUND
ONCE A WEEK
THE SUNNY SIDE

Novels

THE RED HOUSE MYSTERY
TWO PEOPLE
FOUR DAYS' WONDER

Essays

NOT THAT IT MATTERS
IF I MAY
BY WAY OF INTRODUCTION

Children's Books

WHEN WE WERE VERY YOUNG
WINNIE-THE-POOH
NOW WE ARE SIX
THE HOUSE AT POOH CORNER

General

PEACE WITH HONOUR
AUTOBIOGRAPHY

and Several Volumes of Plays

BEHIND THE LINES

BEHIND THE LINES

A BOOK OF POEMS BY

A. A. MILNE

NEW YORK

E. P. DUTTON & CO., INC., PUBLISHERS

To my affinity:

C. R. Milne: Mathematical scholar of Trinity:
And: By the time this appears:
With any luck Private in the Royal Engineers

INTRODUCTION

The verses in this book were written in the opening
nine months of the war. My first feeling, when I got them
together and looked at them, was that many of them were
now so outmoded that they would have lost both meaning and interest for the newcomer; but my second feeling
was that the rush of events had taken them beyond that
stage; had rescued them from the gaucherie of the out-of-
fashion, and had brought them into the respectable haven
of History. Here, for what the record was worth, were the
first nine months of the war as they had been felt by one
Englishman in one English village.

And then I remembered Wordsworth. You too will remember that when he wrote some such poem as (I quote
from memory)—

> To me the meanest child that blows
>   Its nose upon its handkerchief
> Is subject for a rhyming prose
>   Pedestrian beyond belief—

he would preface it with a long explanation as to what he
was thinking at the time, and with whom he was walking
(Coleridge, probably), and what part of the Lakes he was
looking at; so that often the explanation was much longer,
and even duller, than the poem. Indeed, by the time one
arrived at the poem one had no heart for it at all. So it

occurred to me that I would write, not a preface, but a postscript to each set of verses, the which could be easily omitted if the reader were in a hurry. In this way the book does become a sort of diary of the war, and a more composite reflection of the author's mind.

Cotchford Farm,
    Hartfield.
June, 1940.

CONTENTS

9

BEHIND THE LINES

DELIVERANCE

He spoke, and all the world was still . . .
   He spoke. The peoples stayed their breath
To learn the Great Dictator's will,
   To hear the issue—Peace or Death.

He speaks. The absent mind records
   Some faint but well-remembered sound:
A mouse behind the creaking boards,
   An apple falling to the ground.

———•·•———

This was my first feeling when war was declared. Does it need explaining? Millions must have felt a similar relief to know that never again would one be afraid of that voice. So the blackmailed must feel when at last he finds courage to come into court. The experience which he is to go through will be horrible, but his soul is his own again.

ADOLF HITLER

Uneasy Corporal, on whom there lies
    No pride of birth, no dignity of mind,
No majesty of soul: for whom no ties
    Link you in simple friendship with your kind;
Too low for honour and too high for love,
    Cold, solitary, in your eagle's nest,
All Germany below, all Heaven above,
    You write your creed beneath your pagan crest:

"All the fair things which homely natures prize,
    Faith, Mercy, Gentleness have had their day;
Kindness and Pity are but children's cries
    Borne idly on the wind, dying away.
Revenge untaken is revenge abused,
    One grudge forgotten is my Honour's shame,
One lie unspoken is a lie misused,
    One promise kept dishonours my good name."

Uneasy Corporal, with shambling gait,
    Pale hero for a housemaid in her sleep,
Apotheosis of the second-rate,
    Even your wickedness is somehow cheap.

———•———

In the days before the war, when there were many in
England to speak with admiration of Hitler as a Great
Man, I used to say that a man who had never once showed
magnanimity was a second-rate man, and must always remain a second-rate man. He has remained it.

THE THIRD STRING

After years of faithful toil,
Years of soap and years of oil,
After years of saying "Yes,"
Here is Party-Leader Hess.

When (at last) exactly what
Hitler asked for Hitler's got;
When the insistent Goering's dead,
Knifed or knocked upon the head;

When these heroes both depart,
What shall ease the breaking heart?
Who relieve the State's distress?
Surely Party-Leader Hess.

Gallant Party-Leader Hess,
Jotting down the new address,
Hurriedly, in case of trouble,
Advertises for a double.

———•———

It is funny how little we knew about Hess when he was appointed next in succession after Goering. He was Hitler's secretary and Yes-man. It is held by some that the real Hitler died a little while ago, and that one of his doubles is now functioning. Others say that it is a man called Schickelgruber who is causing all the trouble. A third school of thought maintains that Hitler is really Goering, and Goering, Hitler. I never know what to believe.

HIGH PURPOSE

There was a Leader, pledged to burn
With ardour anti-Comintern,
To roll the eye and clench the fist
Against the hellish Bolshevist;
Resolved implacably to purge
All Europe from the Russian scourge . . .

And here the Movement might have stuck
For years, but by a stroke of luck
The Leader's piercing vision saw
The fatal, the almighty flaw:
One vital thing his purpose lacked—
A Russian Non-Aggression Pact . . .

No values die when autocrats
Seal friendship by exchanging hats.
Resolves may function just as grim
Beneath an unaccustomed brim,
And fists be clenched to give expression
(As fervently) to non-aggression.

———————

I defined a Liberal once as "a man who hates Communism and Fascism equally." When Hitler and Stalin joined hands, a great many people suddenly discovered that they were Liberals.

16

AN ALPHABET

A is an Air-raid-precaution. E.g.,
A gas-mask when taking a dip in the sea.

B is my Bicycle. How do you ride it?
I slipped into neutral and sat down beside it.

C is a Curtain. It's thick and it's black,
But a 'plane in the courtyard could see through the
     crack.

D is the Drawing-pins kept for the curtain;
Their *status* is sure, but their *quo* is uncertain.

E is an Elephant. Don't be inferring
It came by mistake: I was thinking of Goering.

F is for Funk. Is it Funk? Is it Frick?
It doesn't much matter. They both make me sick.

G is the Gas-mask I left in the train—
I did it last week, and I've done it again.

H is for— Let us be fair if we can:
He may be all right, but I *don't like* the man.

I's Information, "released" when we know
That all Germany knew it a fortnight ago.

J is the Job which they gave to a Lord
As Censor in Braille to the Fisheries Board.

K was the Kaiser. On both of its fronts
His moustache was the joy of all Germany once.

L is the Lorry I met in the dark,
And (preceded by "Wot the —") the driver's remark.

M is the Milkman. He's surer and surer
Each morning that Itler's been shot by the Furer.

N is for Noah. His mine-laying ark
Was torpedoed by Churchill disguised as a shark.

O is the Organ of Sandy Macpherson.
(I suppose it's all right, and there *is* such a person?)

P is a Pact. One observes with what ease
Any pact is unpact when the pactories please.

Q is Queen Anne, and the Ministry said
She was dying—no, living—no, sorry—she's dead.

R is for Ribbentrop. Isn't he smart?
He has *Rome*—I mean *Moscow*—engraved on his heart.

S is for Stalin. The news has come through
That they've made him an Aryan under Rule II.

T is the Torch which I bought at a sale;
The contact's all right when the batteries fail.

U is the U-boat whose captain convinced an
Unprejudiced Goebbels it must have been Winston.

V is the Voice which announced it. "Here lies"
Is all they need put on its tomb when it dies.

W's Warbles and What-nots. A feller
Is wise, when he hears them, to make for the cellar.

X marks the spot where the body was found
In the books which he reads when he's safe under-
    ground.

Y is the Years (25) which have passed
Since the writer compiled a War Alphabet last.

Z was the Zeppelin, slightly distended,
With which (had you guessed it?) that Alphabet
    ended.

———•———

The Z of that earlier Alphabet was
        Z is a Zeppelin right overhead.
        Isn't it luck to have something for Z?
    Unfortunately one never has anything for X. The only
other one I remember is Q.

Q is the quarrel I had with a man
Who called it Saydong when I called it Sedann.
I call everything Sedann. Try reciting "The Jackdaw of Rahnce," and see where you get.

Reading this Alphabet again six months later I was puzzled by U. Then I saw that the reference was to the Athenia, whose sinking was attributed by Goebbels to Winston Churchill.

THE PORTRAIT GALLERY

Ernst is a farmer, six foot four,
    With enormous feet and a mild blue eye,
And a Hitler plaque on the stable-door
    (And one of Ribbentrop in the sty).

Fräulein Truda is plain of face,
    With a turned-up nose and an empty head,
And busts of Hitler all over the place
    (And two of Goering under the bed).

Hausfrau Hilda's a woman of weight,
    With a face that varies from mauve to pink,
And a portrait of Hitler on every plate
    (And a study of Hess behind the sink).

Hans is a sailor, sailing west,
    Tattooed with an artist's tender care;
There's an excellent Hitler on his chest
    (And a speaking Goebbels I won't say where).

Herr Professor is pinched and small,
    He dines with Anna at half-past-six;
His Fuehrer's figure adorns the wall
    (And the ersatz sausage is wrapped in Frick's).

*   *   *

All these well-established faces
    Fritz has learned to love and know;
Each its chosen corner graces . . .
    But where does Little Red Father go?

———•—•———

The fifth verse leaves me rather ashamed, as if I were hitting a man when he was down. I can see the Herr Professor so clearly. Poor, pathetic, hungry little man. Probably he has invented a new poison-gas, and my sympathy is wasted.

BLACK-OUT

It's hard to know the ins
 And outs of war.
I'd used the drawing-pins
 The night before.

I left them in the wall,
 Or thought I did.
But did I? Not at all.
 They've gone and hid.

Perhaps I took them out
 And put them—where?
Well, somewhere just about,
 Try over there . . .

I put them somewhere *queer* . . .
 Now, wait a bit . . .
I said "I'll put them *here* . . ."
 Of course! That's it!

Now everybody, look!
 I took them, so:
And put them on a book—
 The works of Poe.

Look quick before it's dark—
   It may have been
The Hunting of The Snark . . .
   Well, something green . . .

Was that the night before?
   Or was it not?
Oh, well, we'll have some more,
   I bought a lot.

Don't stand about and hope,
   Just find the tin . . .
Or box . . . or envelope
   I put them in.

They may be lying loose
   Upon a shelf.
Is no one any use
   Besides myself? . . .

*   *   *

Each night the same old argument begins
   We reach the same old impasse every night:
We can't turn on the light without the pins,
   We cannot find the pins without the light.

———•—•———

*The two great annoyances of the early days of the War
(when, unfortunately for England, the War seemed little*

24

more than annoying) were the black-outs and gas-masks. The credit and debit accounts of the black-out must be balanced by others. With gas-masks I had no sympathy— indeed, I had no gas-mask. When the first refugees came beneath my reception-area roof, complete with one gas-mask for a mother and two babies; when they made their first tour of the village with perambulator and one gas-mask, so that the mother anyhow would be safe if Hitler suddenly decided to gas our village; then I did what I rarely do: exerted my authority as Head of the House and forbade her to carry it. I promised her that she shouldn't be gassed while under my care; and, what was more to the point, that she shouldn't starve; for she was supposed to board herself and her children, and had exactly noth- ing a week with which to do it. We managed to get her a compassionate allowance from the authorities, to be paid over to us who were boarding her; so that in a sense we were getting ourselves a compassionate allowance. Well, it didn't matter how one put it, for with so much money in the hand, and a gas-mask doing nothing, she felt the call of London and obeyed it. Later on, the authorities also decided that if an area were certified as "safe" the certificate would command more confidence if the terrors of an immediate gas-attack on it were not over-emphasized. But in those days one had to think of some way of win- ning the war, and gas-masks were easier to make than aeroplanes.

THE HAUSFRAU SPEAKS

Read to me only from thine *Kampf*,
    And I will read from *Mein*,
And we will all our hunger dampf
    For other means to dine.

Great oaks from little acorns came . . .
    Now coffee comes instead;
And sawdust by another name
    Is just as sweet as bread;

The pools of grease, the pools of grease
    Where sizzling bacon sings
Are gone before the hallowed peace
    The Author's Preface brings.

Sound, sound the clarion, fill the fife,
    Proclaim to man and beast
One chapter of our Fuehrer's life
    Is better than a feast.

Long words are more than hamburgers,
    Ay, more than *sauerkraut*,
And simple German faith prefers
    Mein Kampf to getting stout.

Hans Andersen my Johann's brow
    Was like the raven when
He started Chapter One, and now
    He's grey at Chapter Ten.

Say not the struggle gangs agley—
    It gave his hunger spice
To read by accident one day
    The Seventh Chapter twice.

A beetroot by the river's brim
    When stuffed with hips and haws
A tasty sausage is to him
    Who lives by Hitler's laws.

Oh, who will o'er the town with me,
    Oh, who will with me roam
To search for half a pound of tea . . .
    And bring some nettles home.

——— • ———

I was disappointed in Mein Kampf. It was not so illiterate as I had expected. Nor was it so evil. It does not exhibit such a complete negation of human values as is to be found in Rauschning's book Hitler Speaks. I do not see how anybody who has read Hitler Speaks can have any illusion as to the fate of humanity if Hitler conquers. If Hitler conquers, then God (whatever of Goodness, Truth and Beauty each one of us means by God)—then God has lost. This is not a war between nations, but a war between Good and Evil.

27

THE SINKING OF THE
WINSTON CHURCHILL

*You want to see old Joe Goebbels, 'oo scuppered the
    British Fleet?*
*We'll find 'im down at the "Mermaid" at the bottom
    of William Street . . .*
*'Ere, Joe, now tell us the story, the 'ow and the when
    and the where*
You torpedoed the Winston Churchill *with only a
    knot to spare.*

We were lying just off the Banks, boys, with the flood-
    tide rising high,
And all of us there were devil-may-care and ready to do
    or die,
When sudden as death across the Bay an 18-pounder
    barks—
And I blew my tanks and sent to the Banks another
    five million marks.

Then we shortened sail and took the gale abaft of the
    main jib-boom,
And Karl went down to the fo'c'sle hatch and I went
    up to my room.
We'd plotted our course and planned our moves like
    an intricate game of chess,
Which left me time for a gin-and-lime before I was
    due to dress.

There was Fritz at the wheel, and Kurt from Kiel, and
    Karl at the periscope,
And I was having my evening bath and groping round
    for the soap;
The wind was all of it fifty knots and slapping across
    the tide—
And I took the spray in the usual way and then stepped
    out and dried.

We kept one eye on the darkening sky and one on the
    rolling wave;
It was sixteen bells by my old dog-watch, thus giving
    me time to shave.
We'd set our sights for 1,000 yards, and the shells be-
    gan to scream,
As I up and conned my favourite blonde, who was
    looking a perfect dream.

There was Fritz at the wheel and Kurt from Kiel and
    a nice little meal for two,
And we altered our course from time to time as a
    mariner's bound to do;
There was Fritz at the wheel, and Kurt from Kiel was
    manning the forward gun—
And we filled our tanks, and the blonde said "Thanks,
    if it's Bollinger '21."

Then I called for the car and a large cigar, and I called
  for my faithful man
To help me into my fur-lined coat with its collar of
  astrakhan;
And I said good-bye to my lady friend (the women
  come first with me) —
"God rest our souls" (I thought in the Rolls) "who
  earn our bread by the sea!"

The spume flies high in a lurid sky and the long grey
  waters moan
As I take my fur-lined overcoat off and step to the
  microphone.
I clear my throat and a bell-like note goes echoing
  down the air . . .
And that's when I sank the *Churchill*, boys, with only
  a knot to spare.

——————•—•——————

These were the days when Lord Haw-haw was asking
us every night, "Where is the Ark Royal?" There was a
time when the B.B.C. used so much air-space in begging
us not to listen to its rival that I, who had stopped in
boredom long before, began to listen again. But I still
couldn't understand why he was considered such a men-
ace; nor why he had ever been thought funny. Like any
thick-necked man trying to be sarcastic, he was just a
weariness.

SONG FOR A SOLDIER

I march along and march along and ask myself each
    day:
If I should go and lose the war, then what will Mother
    say?
The Sergeant will be cross and red, the Captain cross
    and pink,
But all I ever ask myself is, What will Mother think?

      For
      I
      Kissed her at the kitchen door,
      And promised her as sure as sure
      I'd win the what d'you call it war—
         "You wait," I said to Mother.
      She said, "You mean you'll win the war?"
      I said, "By next September, sure—
      "Why, that's what I'm enlisting for"
         I told my dear old Mother.

She said, "Oh next September, well that isn't very
    soon:
"You know that Father's birthday's on the 28th of
    June?"
I hadn't thought of Father, so of course I had to say:
"All right, all right, I'll win it by the 31st of May."

So

I

Kissed her at the kitchen door

And promised her as sure as sure

I'd win the something something war,

   "You wait," I said to Mother.

She said, "You mean you'll win the war?"

"The end of May," I said, "for sure—

"Why, that's what I'm enlisting for"

   I told my dear old Mother.

She said, "Well that's a comfort; I suppose you hadn't
    heard

"The twinses have their birthday—always had—on May
    the 3rd?"

I wiped away the tear-drop that was flowing down her
    cheek,

And said, "All right, all right, all right, we'll make it
    Tuesday week."

Then

I

Kissed her at the kitchen door

And kissed her once again, and swore

Gort helping me I'd win the war

   To please my dear old Mother.

She said, "You'll really win the war?"
"By Tuesday week?" I said, "For sure,
"And probably the day before"
    I told my dear old Mother.

I march along and march along and hardly dare to
    speak
For planning how to finish off the war by Monday
    week;
For Mother and the Sergeant will be very cross and hot
If we should lose the war because of something I've
    forgot.

    Yes,
    I
    Kissed him at the cook-house door,
    And promised him I'd win the war—
    "Why, that's what I've enlisted for"
        I told my dear old Sergeant.
    He said, "You'll win the ruddy war?"
    I said, "Oh, Sergeant, keep it pure,
    "Of course I'll win the nasty war—
        "And then I'll be a Sergeant."

————•————

This was inspired, if that is the word, by the publication of a marching song whose refrain was "We'll grin,

33

grin, grin till we win, win, win." *I felt so ill after reading it that I had to write this (as I hoped) less nauseating one for myself. In the happy Peace days there was a song much sung in cabarets, and still, unfortunately, to be heard on the wireless, about a lady who wanted some kind gentleman to see her home:* "Me and my dog, Lost in the fog." *I seemed to see the author rushing to his desk one morning, under the shock of the discovery, which had come to him in the night, that* "dog" *rhymed with* "fog." *Only so can the presence of the dog be explained. Only so can the embarrassing presence of that grin be explained.* "Grin" *rhymes with* "win"; *don't waste it.*

UNITY

Herr Hitler rose a little late
And told the Chief of Staff to wait . . .
And sent for him at half-past eight
   And ordered an attack.
The Chief of Staff replying "When?"
And adding "Not by half-past ten?"
The Fuehrer took his fountain-pen
   And wrote him out the sack.

So far the day was going well:
He drew a walnut from its shell
And breakfasted, and rang the bell
   And ordered up the *clique*.
And Goebbels, Himmler, Frick and Hess,
And Ribbentrop and Ley and—yes,
Stout Goering in his fancy-dress
   Arrived to hear him speak.

"My faithful friends," Herr Hitler said—
And wished that one or two were dead
And Goering's neck were not so red—
   "My trusty friends and true,
I do not want to make a speech"—
("*Mein lieber Gott!*" said each to each,
And felt for anything in reach)—
   "The Time has come to Do!"

"Do *whom?*" thought Goebbels with a grin.
But Himmler thought he meant "Do in,"
And rather hoped one might begin
 With Ribbentrop, the swine.
And Ribbentrop, who felt inside
Exactly what that look implied,
Hummed in a careless way and tried
 To think about his wine.

"Now, as our Aryan Shakespeare taught,
By action not by sicklied thought
The Ship of State is safely brought
 To harbours strange and rich.
Be bloody, bold and resolute!"
And Frick, who didn't give a hoot
For Shakespeare, thought: "This means the boot
 For one of us, but which?"

"Good fortune in our fight attends
Brave men who rise to reach their ends
On stepping-stones of their dead friends—
 Who dies if Hitler stands?"
And Goebbels in a wild surmise
Kept thinking to himself "*Who* dies?"
And caught the look in Goering's eyes,
 And half put up his hands.

"Be rich in action, rich in deed,
And suit the action to the need;
Be rich in faith that men succeed
    Who take the lonely way.
Be rich, not gaudy." With an oath
The faithful Goering, who was both,
Scowled at Herr Hess who, nothing loth,
    Scowled at the faithful Ley.

"Now go, my faithful friends. Rejoice
That God has given me the choice
Between—" And suddenly his voice
    Rose to a maddened shout:
"Be off! Your faces make me sick!
And Goering's neck is *much* too thick!
It's bad enough to look at Frick,
    But *Ribbentrop*—! Get out!"

Herr Frick decided not to stay,
Goebbels and Goering said "Good day,"
Hess, Himmler, Ribbentrop and Ley
    Left hastily for home . . .
And Hitler pulled his forelock back,
And countermanded the attack,
And gave two Admirals the sack,
    And tried to ring up Rome.

———•—•———

The B.B.C. which, in my hearing, has spoken of Hore-Beleesha and Hore-Beleisha: and in another connection, of Attila and Atilla: confounded me a few weeks after this was written by calling the fellow, and persisting thereafter in calling the fellow, Dr Lye. I did see at once that there was a joke here if I had known about it in time, but I also realized that a perfectly good set of verses had been ruined. It was no comfort to reflect that many a German poet must have rhymed Marjoribanks with Deutschland, and been equally sorry afterwards. I only refer to this matter because somebody may be writing to me to say that the name is Lye not Lay. I know, I know.

WAR WORK

If only I'd the power to send
    The Board of Trade to Radley,
It wouldn't take an hour to send
        Radley off to Cheltenham,
        Cheltenham to Marlborough,
        Marlborough to Winchester,
            And Winchester to Eton;

And then when things were slack again
    Or going rather badly,
I'd shift the whole lot back again:
        Eton back to Winchester,
        Winchester to Marlborough,
        Marlborough to Cheltenham,
            And have the Germans beaten.

———•———

In Nelson's phrase—or was it Jellicoe's?
Il faut souffrir pour être bellicose.

INFORMATION

It was officially said
This morning that Queen Anne was dead.

By 10.15 the news as stated
Was generally circulated.
But High Authorities at noon
Perceived that she had died too soon,
And saved a difficult position
By rooting out the Lunch Edition.

To make it clear the B.B.C.
Regretted her demise at 3,
And remedied the fault at 5
By hinting she was still alive,
And concentrating on the person
Of Sandy (organist) McPherson.

A messenger was heard to say
"We'd know about it one fine day;"
A typist said: "It won't be yet,
"And anyhow it may be wet."
The Censors put their heads together
And said there wasn't any weather.

Things being in a state of flux,
And Lord Macmillan's motto "**Lux**

Ex tenebris" (and Lord Camrose's
The ancient riddle "Where was Moses?")
The M. of I. devised a plan
To publicise the *birth* of Anne.

A score of sound economists
Described her little dimpled fists;
Ex-diplomats in courtly prose
Explored the wonders of her toes;
A dozen civil engineers
Wrote memos on her childish tears;

And notes about her party dress
(Intended for the neutral press)
Which indicated by a dash
The colour of her baby sash
Were specially designed to stop
The truth from reaching Ribbentrop.

At 10 P.M. (the Night Canteen
Re-opening) the facts were seen
In true proportion, and at last,
All danger mercifully past,
The news was formally released:
"Queen—(? *ask Censor*) is deceased."

Lord Macmillan was Minister of Information—(what a long time ago that seems)—and Lord Camrose had been called in to help him. It was supposed that all the Ministry's propaganda was written by such experts as are mentioned in the fifth verse. But this was not so. Having placed myself at the Ministry's disposal in September, I was asked to do a very delicate, difficult and (as it seemed to me) important piece of work in a very great hurry. Indeed, it almost looked as if I might have to take a special train to London, clutching the precious manuscript, so as to get it there in time; but luckily it was agreed that the few hours' delay would not matter. I worked at it from morning to night, and got it by post to London the next evening. Three weeks later I was told that "They" (Authority too high to mention by name) had now decided that it wasn't wanted after all. When the war broke out again in May, I wrote to the new Minister and said that I would gladly go on writing anything that wasn't wanted, so long as it was really helping to win the war. The legs of this noble and disinterested offer were neatly knocked away (at the very moment, had I known it, when I was posting my letter) by the Government's requisition of authority to conscript anybody or anything which it wanted. But instead of sending two men round for me with a sack, as Goebbels would have done, the Minister not only gave me every opportunity of being useful, but tried to leave me with the impression that it was I who was doing him an extraordinary kindness. I thank him.

FAREWELL TO BUTTER

Latin or French, it's as you please—
   No, no, it's all the same to me:
In Latin, then, *Quot homines,*
   Tot (so to speak) *sententiae;*
In French, to make the matter plain,
   Chacun—(the accent's up to you:
Moisten the lips and start again)—
   Chacun (that's better) *à son goût.*

It may so be (one never knows)
   My readers are a brainless lot—
There is a brainlessness which shows
   And one which, luckily, does not.
So who can tell? In English, then,
   Devoid of passion, anger, haste,
The words come starkly off my pen:
   One cannot argue about taste.

I'm fond of Butter. There are some
   Love operatic music more.
I do not blame them, let them hum,
   If so they must, the *Tosca* score.
I love my Butter. Those who can
   May hymn, on each succeeding week,
Their preference for *Charlie Chan*—
   I dote on Butter: Let me speak.

There is, as must have been observed,
　　Butter and butter. Mine is salt.
For years my taste has never swerved,
　　My judgment never been at fault.
Saltless: the unrewarding stare
　　One gives to jokes one has not seen.
Salted: I take the morning air
　　As radiant as a May-day Queen.

The ways of Nature still are strange
　　Even to me whose interests,
Like Dr Johnson's, lightly range
　　From *edelweiss* to winter vests.
I know a little of the Law,
　　And something of Queen Anne (deceased);
But this I know not: How we draw
　　Sea-butter from an earth-bound beast.

It may be that a cow will yield
　　My sea-tanged butter only if
She pastures on some spray-blown field
　　That tops a tall tide-riven cliff;
Maybe the milkmaid as she milks
　　Dreams of a sailor-lad; maybe
Her name, so nearly Whelks as Wilks,
　　Gives just that something of the sea.

44

The nearness of a farmyard Drake
   (Or is this asking much too much?)
Might by a natural mistake
   Provide the necessary touch.
More likely that some swallow sings
   Sea-shanties to the brooding cow,
From which sweet harmony there springs
   The flavour—but I know not how.

I know not. And no longer care . . .
   Some craven on an office-stool,
With half an idle hour to spare,
   Plans for his lord another pool.
Ah, me! that by this mad caprice
   Sea-butter joins the Great Beyond,
And leaves me here with axle-grease
   Drawn stagnant from an inland pond.

Farewell to Butter! Strange and sad
   How little now it means to me.
To ration it is but to add
   Fresh insult to deep injury.
Keep, keep your slab of vaseline—
   Be it four ounces or a pound,
I give it to the War Machine
   To make its silly wheels go round.

––––– • –––––

I like Butter. I also like this poem. Strange to discover oneself in a world which could do so easily without either.

THE SUPERMEN

God gave to men of German birth
Authority to rule the earth.
We are—you see it in our face—
The one authentic Chosen Race.
In all the world you will not find
The equal of the German mind.
It puzzles strangers to explain
The wonder of the German brain;
They could not possibly suspect
Such overwhelming intellect.
We have the other virtues too:
We're brave, hard-working, faithful, true;
Our strength of purpose is profound,
Our bodies as our minds are sound.
No grace without, no grace within,
But is of German origin.
We are—it is our German creed—
A race of supermen indeed.

Strange that to people so endowed
The use of thought is not allowed;
That gods so resolute and bold
Must think precisely as they're told;
That men of such colossal brain
Should seek the nursery again.

A race of supermen indeed!
Who may not think or talk or read,
Or hear what all the world has heard,
Till Teacher kindly gives the word.
Their wonder-brains! so ill-designed
To use the functions of the mind
That any thought remotely free
Unsettles the machinery.
One doubtful rumour from the Dutch
(It seems) would disengage the clutch;
One broadcast message from the Turks
Would absolutely crash the works;
One leaflet from a British plane
Would pulverise the wonder-brain!

*　　　*　　　*

The Chosen Race! Thank God that we
Have no Divine authority.
We're men; and old enough to vote,
To turn, if so we wish, our coat,
Remain at work, or go on strike,
Say what we like to whom we like,
Distinguish between Jews and Jews,
Believe or disbelieve the news,
Switch on, and then switch off, the tireless
Romancer on the German wireless.

It's nice to be a simple man,
And not a super-Aryan.
It's pleasanter to be adult
Than reverence the Siegfried cult.
I'm glad my uncolossal brain
Won't take me back to school again.
I'm glad that I can write this verse
Without authority from Nurse.

———•———

Hitler's theory is that the Germans are a super-race, and that other races were only created to serve them. As it is also his theory that he and his associates are super-Germans, divinely appointed to make use of all other Germans, we are faced with the astonishing proposition that, by the design of God, all the processes of Creation have been working together for millions of years to produce Hitler, Goering, Goebbels, Ribbentrop, Himmler, Frick and Streicher. Murmuring the names to oneself and visualising the faces, one has an uneasy feeling that the means are disproportionate to the end.

SAFETY

I'm fixing up a Friendly Pact
    Of Firm and Mutual Assistance,
By which, if Russia is attacked,
    I watch from a respectful distance;
And Russia, if one threatens me,
Says "Fancy that!" and "Oh, I see."

This Treaty emphasises first
    A lasting pledge of non-aggression:
And Stalin, who had feared the worst,
    No longer harbours the impression
That on some dark and windy night
I may outflank the Russian right.

Next, actuated solely by
    The spirit of eternal justice,
Our boundaries we rectify
    In perfect trust. To show what trust is,
Each party willingly concedes
The safeguards which the other needs.

I'm giving her the Taj Mahal,
    The Ministry of Information,
Part of the rolling-stock at Basle,
    A five years' lease of Down Street Station,
A small hotel in Amsterdam
And naval bases on the Cam.

And Russia gives me in exchange
 An iceberg which she isn't using,
Bits of the Himalaya Range,
 A cruiser which has finished cruising,
All the Pacific Cortez saw,
And ten years' lease of Bernard Shaw.

The Treatȳ has a final clause
 Which many think the most impressive:
"At any time, for any cause,
 Should either party feel aggressive,
This Treaty is in Law and Fact
A Mutual Aggression Pact."

———•—•———

 I had in my mind those Friendly Pacts which had just been concluded with the Baltic States, and the earlier one with Finland which Russia was now implementing with bombs and tanks. The Russian invasion of Finland seems almost forgotten now—except by Finland. At the time it moved me to a deeper indignation, hatred, despair than anything which Germany had done; and the glory of the Finnish defence to an admiration as deep. I wish that it had moved me to something more worthy than these trivial lines.

PAR NOBILE FRATRUM

"Oppressed Minorities," the "Hostile Act"
"Exhausted Patience" . . . and the Broken Pact:
Which is the prettier; Stalin, tongue in cheek,
Or Hitler saying proudly: "My technique!"

———•———

I have often thought that the answer is Mussolini.

THE BRITISH COMMUNIST

When Lenin first at Heaven's command
    Arose from some Swiss hiding-place,
And, taking Trotsky by the hand,
    Crossed Germany by German grace,
Then Holy Russia thanks to them
Became the New Jerusalem.

These Heavenly Twins were now my gods,
    And daily in the larger parks
I faced the most unpleasing odds
    To preach the gospel of St. Marx.
Who trusts in Trotsky can defy
A ripe tomato in the eye.

My trust, it seemed, was premature;
    Something occurred, I don't know what.
Whoever was the Simon Pure,
    Trotsky was definitely not.
Lenin became Utopia's hub,
And Trotsky plain Beelzebub.

It followed that in some degree
    This doubt assailed me in the night:
If Trotsky is the Boorjwarzee,
    Then Lenin isn't always right
Who for so long was never chary at
Proclaiming him the Proletariat.

But when I'd got the facts arranged,
   I faced the future undismayed.
I saw that Trotsky must have *changed*,
   Which showed how right Our Lenin *stayed*.
"Lenin is *always* right!" I shouted,
And wondered how I could have doubted.

So, later, when Our Stalin came,
   I did not hesitate for long:
A god by any other name
   Is as incapable of wrong:
And just as soon as Lenin died
"Stalin is always right!" I cried.

When generals were shot in squads,
   Was I in doubt again? Not I!
They'd bowed the knee to German gods,
   Were traitors and deserved to die.
I spoke of Rats in league with Foxes
In various parks, on various boxes.

And when Our Stalin bowed the knee
   To those same gods, the Russian rat
Became, from being boorjwarzee,
   Completely proletariat,
And German foxes, as I saw,
Were communists by Nature's law.

So all is well, and Stalin's right
   And will be right until he's dead,
And black is obviously white
   If each alternately is red;
A helpful creed, whose only hitch
Is knowing when the one is which.

No longer now I try to weigh
   The rights and wrongs of this and that,
But leave the Thinking for the Day
   To some far distant Autocrat,
And lie in bed and wait to learn
When Father wants us all to turn.

And if the traitor Trotsky got
   His second wind and came along
And had the gentle Stalin shot,
   Stalin, I'd know at once, was wrong;
And Trotsky would receive the whole
Subservience of my mind and soul.

———••———

"If there were no God, it would be necessary to invent Him," said Voltaire. *This explains why so many people, from quite reasonably clever men like Shaw down to complete fools like Ribbentrop have found it necessary to invent the legend of a Dictator's infallibility. For them Hitler, Stalin or Mussolini is God. He moves in a mysterious way his wonders to perform—in Poland, Finland or Abyssinia; and it is blasphemy to doubt that it is all part of the Great Plan, and for Humanity's benefit.*

54

TRAVEL

Far be it from a Briton to disparage
   Anything born of Commons, Lords and King:
I merely say that in that first-class carriage
   I could not see a thing.

Five shapes were there already, five dim figures:
   But whether men or women, dark or fair,
Or, if it comes to that, full-blooded niggers,
   I knew not. There they were.

We brooded in a silence strange and solemn,
   Gazing at ghosts which gazed as dumbly back.
Dumbly our Late Night Final's Stop-Press column
   Called to us from the rack.

What thoughts went on behind those hidden faces?
   The shape across the way: for all I knew,
Its braces might have been Lord Nuffield's braces,
   Its brain Lord Nuffield's too.

This form beside me: Was it saint or villain?—
   Colonel (or Private) in some training camp?
If I had said "Good evening, Lord Macmillan,"
   Would it have said "Lord Stamp"?

Was it, I wondered, kind to its relations?
  Did it, I wondered, love its fellow-men? . . .
I wondered even more about the stations
  We stopped at now and then.

One would be mine one day; but how to know it?
  Heard station-names are sweet, but those unheard
And unillumed are hell—or so the poet
  (Keats, I believe) inferred.

We stopped. A form vacated the compartment.
  Somehow it *knew* that this was Hadley Wood
(Or Hurstpierpoint). Some quickening at the heart
    meant
    "Go while the going's good."

We stopped. A "GENTLEMEN," reflected sickly
  Beneath a dim blue light, had made it plain
To one of us (but how?) that this was Bickley
  (Or Bude). He left the train.

We stopped (at BOVRIL, if I got it rightly).
  A voice, accompanied by something stout,
Trod on my foot, apologized politely
  And took its colleague out.

Once more we stopped—this time at PORTERS
     ONLY.
  Mistaking it, perhaps, for Porter's Park,
The fourth man hurried off . . . and left us lonely:
  Two of us, in the dark.

Now I could speak. I hailed the fellow blindly:
  "Excuse me, Sir, I live at Wiveltree—
Is it the next but one?" She answered kindly,
  "It *was* the last but three."

———•———

*I used to wonder in these days why nobody called out
the names of the stations in a loud, clear voice. If one
wishes to alight at Wiveltree, and a voice says, loudly
and clearly, "Wiveltree," then one decides that one has
arrived at Wiveltree and one gets out. Or so it seemed to
me. Probably there was a catch somewhere.*

CLASS DISTINCTION

He walked to work on summer days,
   On winter days he took the train.
His "Betters" went their busy ways
   In motor-cars; but he was fain
To trudge upon his own, or stand,
   Strap-hanging, on another's feet—
Not without dust (in summer), and
   (In winter) without heat.

And all the time the thing he hates
   Is class-distinction's ugly sham;
For class-distinction separates
   The automobile from the tram,
And Norman blood from simple trust
   That when these class-distinctions go,
Then no one trudges in the dust,
   Nor shivers at the snow.

The Revolution came to pass
   And ugly class-distinctions went;
With only one surviving class
   So much at least was evident;
And "Gentlemen" who took their ease,
   "Employers" who employed their wits,
And all "Capitalists" like these
   Drove no more to the Ritz.

So "Workers" blessed their lucky star,
    And hugged this comfort to their souls:
That Stalin had the caviare
    And Comrade Hitler had the Rolls,
That Goebbels had the country seat
    Where lovely jewelled ladies shone,
That Revolution was complete
    And class-distinction gone.

*   *   *

He walks to work on summer days,
    On winter days he takes the train.
His "Leaders" go their lordly ways
    In motor-cars; but he is fain
To trudge upon his own, or stand
    Strap-hanging, on another's feet—
Not without dust in summer, and
    In winter without heat.

I have never understood the Class War. I remember reading a letter in some review by that well-known Communist, John Strachey, who always seemed to be arriving at Ellis Island and leaving it; a letter which denied the Editor's assertion that there was no Class War in England. There was a Class War, Mr Strachey screamed. Then which side was he on? Undoubtedly on the side of the Proletariat. I looked up as many Stracheys in Who's Who as I had time for; a remarkable family, stuffed with baronetcies, old school ties, and orders of the Star of India. And a Strachey and the peasant Stalin were on one side in the Class War, and the Duke of Devonshire and I were on the other. Very odd. What was the answer?

The answer is that every war is a Class War in the sense that it is a war between contending classes of men, distinguished by nationality, philosophy or religion. The pretence of the Communist is that the only antagonism which is worth maintaining is that between the social classes (Gentlemen v. Players—or, rather, Workers); and that Utopia can only be reached by·the extermination of one of the classes. Whether it comforts a man who is being beaten up to know that anyhow the man with the rubber truncheon is no gentleman either, or alternatively that both of them are, I do not know. But I do know that as long as there are political prisons there will be a Class inside and a Class outside; as long as there is less than a car a family, there will be a Class driving and a Class being run down; and that this is Class Distinction.

HOARES DE COMBÂT

If I were a Prime Minister, with Britain's wealth of
        brain
    From which to choose a Cabinet with which to win
        the war,
How fatal to our fortunes not to congregate again
    The dear old Party faces I had doted on before!

If I were a Prime Minister and looking for a team
    Of Britain's Greatest Statesmen with the Guts to
        win the war,
How fatal to our fortunes but how easy it would seem
    To overlook Lord Stupid and omit Sir Thomas Bore!

———•———

"Political success,"
        Said Addington to Pitt,
"One ventures to express
        As nascitur, non fit."

———•———

One evening, many months later, it was announced by
the B.B.C. that the Prime Minister had called a meeting
of Defence Ministers, which lasted an hour and a half;
and I thought to myself "And who cares anyway?" Then
suddenly I remembered that Winston Churchill was now
Prime Minister. The news instantly became thrilling. It
seemed possible that that very meeting had won the war.

EXCELSIOR

The shades of night were falling fast
When through a Cornish village passed
A youth who carried in the rain
A placard with the odd refrain,
"Excelsior!"

       I write it thus
Because the Censor made a fuss.
He said "Good heavens, look at this!
An *Alpine* village! That's the Swiss!
This chap of yours appears to be
Infringing Swiss neutrality!"

"You know," I said, "there's just a chance
This Alpine village was in France."

"Geography," the man replied,
"Is for the Censor to decide.
But even if the place were French,
There'd be an observation trench,
A listening-post, or what you will,
Sited on some convenient hill.
And now you're going to tell the Huns
Exactly where to train their guns!"

I said, "This youth, for what it's worth,
Was an American by birth."

The Censor quivered in his chair:
"That's right," he said, "now tell them where
And when America comes in!
D'you *want* the enemy to win?"

I said, "Your pardon, gentle Sir!
Pick any village you prefer."

The Censor scratched a thoughtful head:
"Try Moreton-in-the-Marsh," he said.
"It's good," said I, "but doesn't fit."
"Well, keep the East Coast out of it."
I promised him I wouldn't rest
Until I'd got it in the West.

The Censor groaned and wiped his brow.
I said, "Well, what's the matter now?"
The Censor said "My sainted aunt!
You can't, you absolutely *can't*
Go chattering about the *snow!*"
"Can't you?" I said. "I didn't know."
"Good Gort!" he said, "you've done it *twice!*"
I said the second one was ice.
He cried, "But snow and ice together
Is *telling* Germany the weather!"

"Your pardon, Sir," I said again,
"We'll have a thaw and make it rain."
"That's right," he said, "but don't imply
A fixed condition in the sky."

The Censor wasn't happy yet:
"A point," he said, "of etiquette—
This chap of yours, this feller bore
A *banner*— Now in modern war
It isn't done. At Waterloo
My Uncle Henry carried two;
At Inkerman, I recollect,
We still considered it correct;
But when we come to Spion Kop
Or Omdurman—" I shouted "Stop!
This isn't meant to be the *truth*,
It's *poetry*, about a youth
Who didn't fight in any war,
But simply said 'Excelsior!' "

The Censor looked a shocked surprise:
"You mean," he said, "you're telling *lies?*"
"Well, yes and no," I said: "you see,
It's Longfellow, it isn't me."
The Censor went into a dream . . .
Then murmured "Longfellow? I seem

To know the feller somehow. What's
His regiment—the Royal Scots?
I knew a chap in Poona once—
Is this the Longfellow who *hunts*?"

I said, "No matter, let it go:
I'm leaving out his ice and snow."
"That's right," he said, "and leave his rank
And regiment completely blank."

The shades of night were falling fast
When in the corridor I passed,
While hurrying to catch my train,
A liftman with the odd refrain,
"Excelsior, or Going Down!"
I took the lift and left the town.

———•———

It was only when I wrote about Italy that the Censor's
eye was turned reproachfully in my direction. For months
we had been told that Mussolini was a Stern Realist, un-
moved by sentiment, who would take that precise part
in the war, at that precise moment, which seemed to
offer him the greatest material advantage. But there also
seemed to be a strong conviction in official circles that
he was continually expecting some insult from me which
could only be wiped out by the complete dislocation of
his plans. "I'll come in on June 10th," he was supposed
to have promised Hitler, "always provided that Milne
doesn't call me a gangster before then." I could never
quite believe this.

MERRY CHRISTMAS

Pile on the logs, the wind is chill,
But let it whistle as it will,
We'll keep our Christmas merry still.*

On these occasions Reason goes
Where Fancy leads her— I propose
To wear a long fictitious nose;

To this I add (in flaxen crêpe)
Some whiskers of romantic shape
Tied firmly to the ears with tape.

Accoutred thus, I mean to be
A source of simple gaiety,
A fount of laughter. We shall see.

It is, I rather think, at meals
My sense of humour best reveals
That subtle art which art conceals.

The parlourmaid, although denied
By act of war the old and tried
Assistance of a butter slide.

* This verse, I ought to say, is not
My own unaided work, I got
A hint or two from Walter Scott.

66

Has still a merry laugh in store:
A string across the kitchen door
Enables her to take the floor.

For friends I have some Jolly Jestes
Which, long experience attests,
Unloosen the most costive guests:

I've fashioned after anxious weeks
An egg for hardier physiques
Which, when decapitated, *shrieks*;

The fairer sex will merely cope
With salted almonds made of soap:
A whimsical surprise (I hope);

And, for the elderly, I think
We'll serve that rather *subtle* drink
Which *looks* like port and *is* red ink.

So taking it all round, you see
My Christmas is designed to be
A day of mirth and jollity.

And all my actions will be graced
By whiskers and (in perfect taste)
A nose which reaches to the waist.

*   *   *

Pile on the logs, the wind is chill,
But let it whistle as it will,
We'll keep our Christmas merry still:

Such was my hope. But world affairs
So held me that a flight of stairs
Came on the Thinker unawares . . .

Pile on, O medico, your bill
And whistle for it as you will—
At least I kept my Christmas still.

———————

This was the first and, as I am hoping, the only Christmas of the war. In the last war we began saying in 1914 that the war would be over by Christmas. We went on saying it until 1918; and in 1918, as was inevitable sooner or later, we were right. And so this time I have been saying that the war will be over in November; no, I never thought November, 1939; November, 1940. This is June, 1940, and I still say so. Somehow it seems more likely to be right than if I said it would be over by Christmas.

OBSESSION

Goebbels, thou shouldst be lying at this hour—
   Get busy, Goebbels; greet the glad New Year,
Not with a face that makes the milk turn sour,
   But one that brings fresh bubbles to the beer;
Smile, and step smartly to the microphone
And give the boys a good one: all your own.

What mighty ills have not been done by Churchill!
Who was't betrayed the Capitol? Why, Churchill!
Who lost Mark Antony the world? Just Churchill!
Who was the cause of the long ten years' war,
And laid at last proud Germany in ashes?
(*Sorry. Correct*)—and laid old Troy in ashes?
Destructive, damnable, deceitful Churchill!

     Who is Silvia? What is she
       That the Jews have bought her?
     Silvia is known to be
       Winston Churchill's daughter.
     She is now a British spy
     With a most come-hither eye,
     And the length of Silvia's lashes
     Causes all those railway crashes.

Who gassed the Princes in the Tower and starved them
      by blockade?
Who put the nitro-glycerine in Borgia's lemonade?

Who sank the schooner *Hesperus?* And why and why
    and *why*
Did *all* of Thomas Moore's gazelles mysteriously die?
Whose was the most unkindest cut in Caesar's Sunday
    suit?
And who deliberately made the rift within the lute?
Who trained the asp to coil itself in Cleopatra's lunch?
Who poisons little children's minds with ribald verse
    in *Punch?*
Research has found the answer. All these innocents
    have bled
To satisfy the lust of Winston Churchill's Uncle Fred.

    As intercepted letters show,
    Guy Fox, the beast who tried to blow
      Our Reichstag to the skies,
    Was not a fox at all. No, no,
    But Winston Churchill's Auntie Flo
      In sinister disguise.
    His *favourite* aunt, suborned by Jews
    (Tell all the boys. They'll *eat* the news).
    Who killed Cock Robin? Whose the nest
      From which was pressed the fatal trigger?
    No sparrow's, but the gilded perch
      Of Mr Churchill's Budgerígar.

With news like this to bring the New Year in
You'll be a riot, Goebbels, in Berlin.
Give us a song! "Who Loves to Lie With Me?"
(On, how appropriate, the dirty Spree).

———•—•———

Poetry makes stern demands of its votaries, and it demands here that you should pronounce "budgerígar" to
rhyme with trigger, and think of it, if you must, as a
different bird from the budgerigár to which you are ac-
customed; a bird, let us say, shorter in the body and
longer in the tail. Thank you.

HOME SERVICE

Fas est—which means it's always wise—
Ab hoste—from our enemies—
Doceri—to annex or pinch
Any idea which seems a cinch.
To which I add *Festina lente:*
Don't do it till you've counted twenty.

It's commonly accepted by
The thoughtful jurist (such as I)
That punishment should fit the time,
The circumstances and the crime.
The facts, the local situation,
Demand profound consideration
Before the jurist can begin
To calculate the price of sin.
But we distinguish as a rule
Between the villain and the fool;
And since, by general accord,
True virtue is its own reward,
So folly may itself provide
Such sentence as should be applied.

These are the reasons why I think
That Parliament is right to shrink
From making death the penalty
For listening to the B.B.C.

It's Folly, not a Major Sin,
Week after week to listen in
To some unenterprising bore
Who tells you what you knew before.
There may be some—there's always this—
Whose ignorance can make it bliss;
To hang them, foolish as they are,
Is going, surely, *much* too far.

But men who have for stock-in-trade
A husky voice that's overlaid
With alcohol, and interlaced
With aitches doggedly misplaced,
Convinced that they are giving so
A "little Cockney cameo";

And women who impersonate,
In accents wildly out of date,
Some false, imaginary char
And make you wonder *what* they are:
If the authorities should find
These contraband, I shall not mind.

And if they thoughtfully instal
Death penalty by axe for all
Who have (and boast about it) "RHYTHM,"
Then I am *definitely* with 'em.

———•———

In the good old days of singing, the singer followed the tune in words so little recognizable as words that even the language of them was not easily to be identified. The modern method is to make a real acting performance of the words, and to let the tune, if we may call it so for the moment, keep in step as best it can. In a passion of reverence for the theme the "singer" tells us that

> When the moon swinging high
> Shone down on you and I,
> Love came into my heart
> And I knew that death could not us part.

It is terribly moving if you don't happen to mind how emotions are expressed, so long as they are good ones; but to a writer who doesn't mind what anyone is expressing, so long as he is expressing it well, it is an agony. All songs should be hummed. Modern songs should be unaccompanied and hummed on one note.

THE BOTTLE

There is a well-house by the cottage door,
    A plain small house, devoid of decoration;
And visitors who have not been before,
    Mistaking it for "outside sanitation,"
Avert the head politely, till we tell
The silly creatures that it is a well.

Within, spring water rises, cool and clear;
    But holes and runs, which probably a mouse made,
Admit the local fauna. It was here
    An unresponsive grass-snake met the housemaid.
She dipped and drew it in her pail, and got
A frosty look which plainly said: "So what?"

So what? . . . We gourmets have our separate codes.
    One draws the line at beetles, and another,
Who hates to split a drink with frogs and toads,
    Will toast the water-boatman as a brother.
If no one cared for snakes (and no one cared)
Then snakes were off. I had the place repaired.

And it was so I learned about The Day.
    For when the reconstruction work was ended,
I gave the thing a casual O.K. . . .
    Two shelves are built above the well, intended
For use as larder. On the upper shelf
A *bottle gleamed*. I saw it there myself.

It was the true, the blushful Bollinger!
    (Blushing to find itself down here in war-time)
And '29, the vintage I prefer,
    But in the country had not known aforetime.
"Who's drinking *this*?" I cried. "And *when*?" I said.
The answer came: "Why, Us—when Hitler's dead."

And suddenly I saw in every cot
    And every castle people celebrating
In Beer or Bollinger (it mattered not)
    The Day for which a heart-sick world is waiting.
"The Beast is dead!" a million voices shout.
"Where is that bottle? Bring that bottle out!"

———— •—•————

*One would have liked another bottle for Mussolini,
but perhaps he is hardly important enough.*

WEATHER REPORT

The home thermometer last night
    Went down to 4 and stayed,
Doing all this by Fahrenheit
    And not by Centigrade;
Subtracting 4 from 32
    One estimates with ease
We had a frost the whole night through
    Of 28 degrees.

The war has spoilt a lot of things:
    We're full of "rights" and "wrongs;"
And almost everybody sings
    The most appalling songs;
But what infuriates me most
    Is simply that I've lost
The opportunity to boast
    About my "record" frost.

For in the happy days of old
    One scanned the news to see
If Littlehampton were as cold,
    Or Looe as hot, as we.
But now comparison is gone—
    Not least of Hitler's crimes
Is that he put the kybosh on
    The weather in *The Times*.

77

Ah me! those spirited reports
   ("Sunny A.M., but cool")
From all the popular resorts—
   E.g., from Pontypool.
How much allure a breakfast lacks
   Unable to begin
With temperatures *min.* and *max.*,
   Particularly *min.*

I crack the still unrationed egg,
   I carve the rationed ham,
I know it's cold in Winnipeg
   And cold in Amsterdam;
I munch the sparsely-buttered toast,
   I stir the tasteless tea,
But know not (what intrigues me most)
   The *min.* at Brightlingsea.

The home thermometer went down
   To 4; it really did.
Can Colchester or Camden Town
   Produce a lower bid?
Thermometers at Heckmondwike
   Of similar design—
Can *they* show *mins.* remotely like
   This *minimum* of mine?

Penarth and Peebles, what of them?
　　They have their frosty spells;
And doubtless it is "cold A.M."
　　At Troon and Tunbridge Wells;
It may be that at Aldershot
　　A heat-wave has begun.
I doubt it. But it matters not—
　　The war has spoilt the fun.

So, just to keep the record right,
　　I'll mention it once more:
The home thermometer last night
　　Went firmly down to 4.
Which 4 must stand alone. Ah, me!
　　The triumph I have missed with
No hopeful 5 from Bridge of Dee,
　　No 6 from Aberystwyth!

———◆———

We have two thermometers: a personal one just out-side the garden door, and a working one by the potting-shed. This makes it more exciting; because when I tell the gardener that we had sixteen degrees of frost last night, he will say, with pride ill-concealed, that he had twenty. This may be because he is further removed from sea-level than we are, or because his thermometer is younger and more susceptible. There is also a pleasing variation in our own thermometer. I mean that the right-hand side which goes up is always lower than the left-hand side which goes down; so that it is four degrees colder—I may have to break off for a moment and verify all this, but I don't want to if I needn't—so that it is three degrees hotter—well, assume that the left-hand side is numbered one way, I can't remember which for the moment, and the other side the other way, then that means— What I feel is that if I do stop, then I shan't go on again, I shall become apathetic about the whole thing . . . Oh all right, we both are. Anyway the two sides are different, and so, I suppose, are the gardener's two sides, so that we have four temperatures every day; which, as I said, is much more exciting.

Our barometer fell off its hook some months ago, and went down to "Stormy." It stayed there so long that I feared it had lost interest. Not so. Helped by a cloudless week of calm weather, it got its second wind (so to speak) and crawled up to "Very Wet." A further month's drought brought it triumphantly to "Rainy." In short, as Galileo said, "It moves," which is enough for any barometer. Making the proper allowances, and taking the merest peep out of the window, we know what the weather is up to.

ALMOST A GENTLEMAN

Dear Reader (may I call you Friend?),
I've asked the Editor to lend
His columns to me. Please attend.

I am a plain bluff man—the sort
You British call a "perfect sport,"
An "English gentleman," in short:

Who shoots the fox, and hunts the boar,
And keeps the beaters in a roar
With jokes they may have heard before;

Who likes his glass, but not beyond
The second bottle, and is fond
Of pretty women (mostly blonde);

An honest man, devoid of craft,
Who's lived for sport, and loved and laughed;
A man of substance—fore and aft;

Such as an Englishman would term an
"Awfully good feller for a German"—
That's yours sincerely. Call me Hermann.

Well, here we are. Our common goal
Is Peace—and then some rigmarole,
To save our face, about the Pole.

Forget about the Poles and Czechs!
For you and me to save our necks
One man is wanted: *Hermann Rex.*

Adolf, poor fellow, doesn't play
"The cricket," as we sportsmen say—
Besides, he's crackers anyway.

You cannot trust him. I will see
To Adolf and some fifty-three
Of Adolf's yes-men . . . leaving Me.

Then, I and you, dear Readers, go
To London, Paris—yes-or-no?—
And make a little Treaty. So.

We save our cash, we save our necks,
We talk about the Poles and Czechs,
And seal and sign it: "Hermann Rex."

So all's as friendly as can be,
And I am made by State decree
A member of the M.C.C.

(P.S.—Excuse for talking shop:
Does any reader care to swap
A stomach-pump for Ribbentrop?)

———•·•———

I am always puzzled to understand why the Almost a Gentleman type can so easily break down the barriers of the fastidious. Lord Halifax, for instance: the highest type of Christian Englishman: let him stand for all that we mean by "English gentleman"; he fell (and there are some who can never forgive him for it) he fell for Goering. He was dismayed by no blood on the hand held out to him, by no coarseness in the manners of the Perfect Sport with whom he shared a taste for killing small animals. "A sportsman and almost a gentleman"—like that Prince of Crooks, Horatio Bottomley, whose hand, also, was never refused. It's funny.

SLEEP NO MORE

You have not slept? Why should you sleep
   When all the unrequited dead
Rise from their lowly graves to keep
   A nightly vigil round your bed?

Heil Hitler! These who seem to live
   Are those you scourged and crucified.
Their faces frighten you? Forgive
   Their faces—that is how they died;

Heil Hitler! And the hand that falls
   Is ugly with unhealing scars
From scratching "Justice!" on the walls,
   From beating at the prison bars.

Heil Hitler! From a conquered land
   They come to herald you, for whom
A hundred thousand crosses stand
   To mark your German "living room."

Heil Hitler! On the air is borne
   That doleful, thin, unending cry
Of women from their homesteads torn
   And left in frozen fields to die.

They rise from long-forgotten graves,
    They fill the shadows round your bed,
Dead souls of all your living slaves,
    The living souls of all your dead.

How should you sleep? That ghostly wake
    Will hold you till the long night ends
(*Heil Hitler!*) and the shadows take
    The likeness of familiar friends.

They greet you, they have served you well:
    The bully, the corrupted youth,
The lackey with no soul to sell,
    The pygmy who has murdered Truth.

———•———

In some speech made at this time Hitler said that he had been working day and night for the good of his people, and had not slept since the war began.

THE NEUTRAL

It's grand to be an Autocrat:
To tell the people "That is that!"
And hear them fervently express
Their faith in it by shouting "Yes!"
It's also very pleasant not
To hear them asking "What was *what?*"
As men will ask each other, who
Have somehow missed the vital clue.
No autocrat requires to fear
The things he doesn't wish to hear;
What only matters is to say
"Pom! Pom!" and have them shout "Hooray!"

So when a great decision rests,
Not poised within a million breasts,
But on the will of one alone,
It's nice to know the will's your own;
And, once decided, nicer still
To know it's now The People's Will.
And if the issue's "Peace or War,
And *Which* Side are we Fighting For?"
The Autocrat's importance thrives
From toying with a million lives,
From seeing that a nation's soul
Is fixed upon *his* chosen goal.
Does he assist the "Plutocrats"?

Then all the people raise their hats,
And forty million minds agree
There's nothing like Plutocracy.
Or does he smile upon the Reds?
Then all the people bare their heads,
And forty million bodies bend
In homage to The Workers' Friend.

So, when the Great Decision comes,
And men fall in behind the drums,
And music sets their hearts aflame
To fight, and die, for—whatsitsname?
Then may no warrior forget
The cause on which his soul is set;
May none, anointed for the fight,
Cry vaguely "God defend the Right—
Or possibly the Left," because
He can't remember which it was.

In 1926 the man with whom I had just been playing golf said to me: "You know, we want somebody like Mussolini over here." I said coldly: "Oh? Do you like murderers?" For Mussolini had murdered Matteotti. At the beginning of this war I wrote to a friend who had referred to this murder in his latest book: "Glad to see you remember Matteotti. I thought I was the only Englishman who did." At the beginning of this war I wrote in a letter to The Times (and subsequently in articles else-

where) that if this were a war to end war it must be a war to re-establish democracy in Europe. This had the distinction of annoying Signor Gayda, who said that it was a deliberate attack on Italy; and an English editor was found to apologize for me, and to explain to Signor Gayda that he mustn't mind what I said, because nobody else did. All through the war I have been trying to say what I thought about Mussolini, and have been hampered by the official view that "we mustn't offend Italy." O God! O Matteotti! Apparently there was still a hope that this murderer and gangster, the breaker of treaties, the ravisher of Abyssinia and Albania, might join us in a war against "the evil things," if sufficiently bribed. Well, just as it is unfair to judge Italy by Mussolini, so is it unfair to judge England up to 1939 by its Government. But in England public opinion can (and, thank God, did) turn the Government out. This is the Democracy for which I think we are fighting. For it is the common man, not the statesman, who has ideals.

TALK

Seated one night at the wireless,
  Weary and ill at ease
(The fire was out, and the fireless
  Room had begun to freeze),
I gave a twitch to the needle,
  I pressed the button for "Wave,"
And voices started to wheedle,
  Voices started to rave.

I pottered from Rome to Warsaw,
  I twiddled from Russ to Finn,
And, steering a zig-zag course, saw
  The moon come up in Berlin;
I sauntered from Prague to Oslo,
  I lingered in old Madrid—
And heard, wherever I was, low
  Consonants grate and skid.

I twiddled the "Vol. Controller,"
  I twiddled two knobs as one,
And waves from seas that were Polar
  Joined waves from seas in the sun;
And rivers which rolled from Florence
  In waves which broke at the crest
Met Moscow's thundering torrents
  And trickled to Budapest.

Wherever I stayed the needle,
    However remote the shore,
A face would whinny and wheedle,
    A face would bellow and roar.
I could picture it flushed and sweating,
    I pictured it tense and white,
I said "And I wouldn't mind betting
    It's just what he said last night."

A hundred vehement faces,
    Sallow and flushed and fat,
Telling you what the case is
    For this and the other and that . . .
And every night at eleven,
    As sound streams up to the skies,
Truth listens-in from Heaven
    And climbs on her Cross, and dies.

———◦•◦———

I can understand that the German Government finds
it necessary to exhort the German people every two hours:
"Under our great Leader we march to Victory. Yesterday
we sank the last six English battleships, leaving only
seventeen to be disposed of. Bark scrapings make a good
substitute for coffee. Anybody who doesn't will be shot."
For it is the German Government's war. But here it is
the British people's war, and it is we who should be exhorting the British Government. I wish that once a week
we could be sure that all Ministers and Civil Servants

were listening in, while we urged on them the need for courage, common-sense, vigour, imagination, and fidelity to the ideals for which we are fighting. We have been told lately to lie down and put our arms over our ears when bombs drop. If the Conservative Party had adopted this position for the last few years when Hitler was proclaiming himself its bulwark against Bolshevism, we should feel much safer now.

OFFICERS AND GENTLEMEN

Karl Harkoff was an Englishman of credit and renown,
He had a little place in Kent, a maisonette in Town.
Lew Russky was a Highlander, he travelled to and fro:
And everywhere that Russky went, his Rolls was sure
    to go.

A gentleman called Judah said: "I'm making mar-
    malade,
Or would if I'd a factory, and knew how it was made.
And then I'd want some capital and lots of working-
    men—
This whisky's pre-the-last-war . . . Just a little one? Say
    when."

And Captain Russky answered: "I can find you all the
    cash
At 10% commission, but it might be rather rash,
Unless you had a letter from the Ministry to say
They'd like a lot of marmalade on such-and-such a day."

So Judah went to Harkoff, and when compliments
    were paid,
Said "Listen, I've a factory for making marmalade.
The capital is ample, we can make it by the ton—
I wondered if . . . No, not for me . . . Well, just a
    little one."

And Captain Harkoff answered: "I can get you if you
    wish
An order for a thousand tons at 10% commish . . .
And if you have a cousin who would like a second star,
He can have it for a 'monkey' . . . Second cousin? Right
    you are."

Then Judah said to Harkoff: "Now about this mar-
    malade:
It's messy stuff to handle and I don't know how it's
    made.
Suppose I sold the contract to a man who makes the
    stuff—
Would 10% commission (fifty-fifty) be enough?"

And Captain Harkoff answered: "Well, if that refers
    to me,
I know the very man you want, a traveller in tea;
An open-minded sort of cove, who doesn't give a
    damn—
He'd travel just as happily in marmalade and jam."

So Judah went to Russky and he said: "About the
    loan:
You needn't bother, Captain, I can do it on my own."
And Major Russky answered: "If it's all the same to
    you,
I'll ring up Major Harkoff and we'll put the matter
    through."

So when the traveller in tea had found a man who made
A lot of Diesel engines, but who *could* make mar-
malade,
They sold him Judah's contract, and (to help the boys
in France)
Took 10% commission and a thousand in advance.

So both the Colonels made a bit and drew a Colonel's
pay,
And Captain Judah made a bit, but not so much as
they;
And since the troops like marmalade and want it more
and more,
These officers and gentlemen have helped to win the
war.

Epilogue

Karl Harkoff is a General of credit and renown,
He has a country seat in Kent, a mammoth house in
Town;
Lew Russky is a General, he travels to and fro,
And everywhere that Russky is, two Rolls are sure to go.

———•—•———

When this first appeared, I was accused by two or
three people of "attacking Jews." This was only because
one of the characters was "a gentleman called Judah." I

had hoped that nobody was called Judah. It is admirable, and yet rather pathetic, this feeling which Jews have about each other: that an attack on one of them is an attack on all of them. Chartered accountants never feel like this about chartered accountants. A dramatic critic did once write that all dramatic critics were unprejudiced and intelligent (I don't know where he got the idea from), but even he wouldn't resent it as an insult to his calling, if an imaginary critic were depicted as a wife-beater. Anyway, these verses are not an attack on Jews, but an attack on lice.

MATILDA

The Fall of Man was due to Eve.
   Of Troy? A woman made it fall so.
A woman, in his heart close-curled,
Lost poor Mark Antony the world . . .
To these Destroyers, by your leave,
   I add Matilda also.

When I was young, and Hitler small,
   And Goering hadn't left his hangar,
I went to Norway, having bought
A passage on the *Argonaut*,
A vessel advertised to call
   At Bergen and Stavanger.

We sailed . . . and memory records
   The crossing (which was rather stormy):
Matilda (a delightful blonde
Perched on the deck-rail): and, beyond,
A panorama of the fjords
   Spread lavishly before me.

We reached Stavanger. Did I shout
   "Behold Stavanger! Key to Norway"?
I did not. No, I lay in wait,
In sight of Cabin 28,
And caught Matilda coming out,
   And kissed her in the doorway.

But little more remains to tell . . .
    My memories, which should have filled a
Portentous volume on the place
Regarded as an Air Force Base
"By One Who Knows the Country Well"
    Are centred on Matilda.

How welcome I should be today
    Without that blonde enchantress (curse her)!
The articles that I could write
Were she not always in the light—
The expert knowledge I'd display
    Had she preferred the Purser.

"Norway: Its Letters, Life and Laws";
    This, in a style resembling Gibbon's,
Had been my most important book
(Two volumes), but Matilda took
The pages in her pretty paws
    And tore them into ribbons.

With one Matilda overboard,
    One blonde the less (confound and hang her),
Your Special Representative
Would now be hastening to give
The low-down on the Oslo Fjord,
    The Truth about Stavanger.

———•———

How far away Norway seems now! The hopes we had from it, the disappointments we suffered! But let it always be remembered that it was not to Norway that Mr Chamberlain referred when he said that Hitler had missed the bus. As he explained to the House of Commons on May 9th, he was referring to the Western Front.

SPRING OFFENSIVE

My Muse, though anxious to discuss
   "The Spring Offensive: Where? And When?"
Agrees that it is not for us
   To drive too ponderous a pen.
So, therefore, we proceed to sing,
   Without a "By your leave" or "Pardon,"
About the most offensive spring
   Which occupies the garden.

There is, of course, a Spring as sung
   By poets in immortal song
Too much recited by the young,
   With all the intonations wrong;
A Spring which, in the poet's mind,
   Is always (somehow) doing nicely;
The one which isn't far behind
   If Winter comes. Precisely.

And Winter came. No hope to hide
Its havoc, or avert the blame.
Six Censors standing side by side
   Would see at once that Winter came.
Six Censors standing in a row
   Would pass for instant publication
The casualty lists which show
   The Winter's animation.

Wordsworth, a man of simple tastes,
    Would give no cottage garden up
Which bore amid its blackened wastes
    One unpretentious Buttercup.
He found "the meanest flower" divine;
    He was, to take an instance, crazy
Upon the Lesser Celandine,
    And crackers on the Daisy.

For me, alert to Nature's spell
    But with responses more controlled,
The Hairy Pokeweed rings no bell,
    The Bulbous Crowfoot leaves me cold.
It was for Wallflowers, warm and gay,
    Now withered, that my soul was thirsting . . .
I merely look the other way
    When told the Bugwort's bursting.

Yet hope is not completely dead;
    Amid grim spaces, bleached and bare,
The Polyanthus lifts a head,
    And Daffodils are here and there.
My loved Rock-roses may be Hel—
    (Wait for it, madam) Helianthemum,
But in the autumn—who can tell?—
    We *might* have a Chrysanthemum.

So much for that. By no intent
    I reach the burden of my song
Five verses later than I meant,
    But still, thank Heaven, going strong.
Chance willed it so. I strive to tell
    In rhyme, if not for any reason,
The truth about a spring (or well)
    And not about a season.

So here it is. Let's get it right.
    A spring beneath the putting-lawn
Which bubbles gaily, day and night,
    From dawn to eve, from eve to dawn,
Has left it a tenacious bog
    Which holds, as far as we can figure,
One ornamental seat, the dog,
    Three golf-balls and a jigger.

———•———

Nevertheless the record for this twelve-hole course, over bog, hill and dale, is two under twos. The record, I need hardly say, is held by myself; otherwise I shouldn't be mentioning it. The real garden-tragedy of the winter was the death of our three best climbing-roses, including that loveliest of all climbers, Mermaid.

QUID PRO QUO

Here's to the Chancellor! Here's to you, Simon!
   What, are you taking my money away?
Plunder as much as it pleases you. I'm an
   Ardent accessory, just for today.

Ask me for 80 per cent. of my income;
   Double the duties on whisky and beer;
Fine all the finnicky folk who won't drink 'em—
   Stick to it, Simon. I'm ready to cheer.

Rake in the overdue money the slack owe,
   Don't let the dodger escape from your clutch;
Put what you like on my snuff and tobacco—
   Let me support you by smoking too much.

Twopence for letters? Of course I don't grudge it—
   Answering letters is only polite.
Now, for a change, just to balance your Budget,
   Letters are welcome, and answered at sight.

What about Cats? Not the human, the feline—
   Pussies with whiskers, four legs and a tail?
Here we have two of the best. Make a bee-line
   Straight for our cats, and I'll pay on the nail.

Tax every hair on my head, and I'll simply
    Swamp it with lotions to nourish its pores;
Tax every pimple, I'll try to go pimply—
    Anything, Simon, you want shall be yours.

Does this seem odd to you? Well, I'll be frank, you
    Mustn't suppose that I'm touched in the head.
No. It is just that I've got to say thank you . . .
    I am still living—and others are dead.

Younger and better men day after day go
    Proud to their destiny. As for myself,
Sheer middle-age and a touch of lumbago
    Keep me in safety at home on the shelf.

Others are fighting, and Death, ever present,
    Swoops from the sky and spouts up from the seas . . .
What can I do? I can pay and look pleasant.
    Tax me, good Simon, as much as you please.

———◦———

And he did.

GUESTS

Our "refugees" have left us. Since September's
　　First darkened days made light of all our prayers
We had been very close together: members
　　Of one another—mostly on the stairs.

Our refugees are gone. The stairs are wider;
　　Our one spare-room is spare; the housemaid's knees
Are bent on "cleaning up." (This may decide her
　　To stay with us.) Farewell, O refugees!

Paid guests are sweet, but those unpaid are sweeter:
　　True hospitality is "uncontrolled."
Here in the wilds our lives will be completer
　　With friends we chose, and loved, in days of old.

"Shall we have Sheila?" Sheila is a darling—
　　Oh, yes, I love her just as much as you:
A dear . . . but, dash it, chatters like a starling—
　　Just *think* of her at meals. She wouldn't do.

"Let's have the Bretts." A charming pair, though not
　　　　one's
　　Idea of lively company—but *pets* . . .
Oh, wait a bit! They'll *both* want baths, and *hot* ones—
　　A lot of extra pumping. *Not* the Bretts.

"What about Anne?" She'd want to bring her babies.
  As to a housewife seems the Sunday joint,
As to a mariner an astrolabe is,
  So to a mother— Quite. You see the point.

"Shall we have Michael?" No, we won't have Michael.
  How can I work if Michael is about?
He sings. I love him, but he has a cycle
  Of songs he tries to sing. Michael is out.

"Shall we have Henry?" *Far* too fond of butter.
  "John?" Too familiar. "Mary?" Out of touch.
"What about Susan?" Susan doesn't utter.
  "What about Stephen?" Stephen talks too much.

Have Peggy if you like— No, *I* can't stick her . . .
  Oh, nothing, no . . . Oh, certainly . . . Oh, quite . . .
And let's be fair, I *have* seen ankles thicker—
  Once—long ago . . . You *won't* have Peggy? Right.

What about George? . . . Yes, George . . . Well, what's
      the matter?
  What about George was what I said. Why say
What about George? This nigger-minstrel patter
  Just gets us nowhere. George? . . . No George
      today.

Shall we have *no one*— (oh, the peace and quiet!) —
No one who grumbles, no one hard to please,
Nobody wasteful, fussy, on a diet . . .
Shall we (in short) get back our refugees?

———•———

This was our second lot of refugees; a mother and two children of school age. We boarded and lodged them at the Government expense, for the mother was some kind of a "helper" at the school. Later, when so many children returned to London that the mother's services were no longer required (or paid for), the family moved into the village and looked after itself. Their man was a reservist, and a hairdresser by profession. He had been with the B.E.F. from the beginning of the war, and it was generally supposed in the village that, among his other duties, was that of cutting Lord Gort's hair. Naturally we all felt very proud of this. It was as near to Gort as any of us was likely to get. And, if it is not impertinent, I should like to add that he may well have been proud of his children. They couldn't have been nicer.

THE PATRIOT

The weather: One must keep it dark,
   And I was wrong to say,
On rising with the oldest lark,
   "Oh, *what* a lovely day!"
"O all ye little hills, exult!"
I cried aloud on Wednesday *ult.*,
And by this innocent remark
   I gave the show away.

Well, there it was, the day was fine;
   The surest of our clocks
Had fixed the hour (by striking 9)
   At 10.15 approx.,
And by 11 I should be
Caparisoned upon the tee
In trousers of a spring design
   And regimental socks.

At breakfast—and the gods forbid
   The meal I love the most
Should dwindle—there were *(semper id.)*
   Two scrambled eggs on toast.
I ate, and swore "By Slav and Serb
My golf today shall be superb!
I'll play like Cotton," and I did
   An 84 at most.

If I tell Hitler how I made
   The ball pull up and stop
Stone dead at each approach I played,
   Will he tell Ribbentrop?
Shall Goering know (I think he should)
How accurate I was with wood?
Need any golfer be afraid
   Of talking golfers' shop?

He need not; and no secrets now
   Come oozing out from me,
And when the wind is East by Sou',
   I say it's Sou' by E;
And oh! my lips are tightly sealed
About our forces in the field—
For all I talk about is *How*
   I did an 83.

———◆———

I had arranged to play golf one Friday, and just as I was starting off, the telephone bell rang, and I was told that Germany had invaded Holland and Belgium. So I played . . . and have not played since. I thought of nine good reasons why I should go on playing, and none why I shouldn't. But I couldn't.

OLD SOLDIER

In Britain's last War to end Peace
   I weighed up my country's position
And, knowing the cousin of somebody's niece,
   I applied for (and got) a commission.

I sported a star on my sleeve,
   And then, when the weather was colder,
I added another (with Kitchener's leave)
   And the two were stitched on to my shoulder.

Myself and platoon were as one:
   There's much I could rightfully say on its
Response when I gave it the order to "shun"
   And mark time and form fours and fix bayonets.

My voice was the sergeant's delight,
   Each man in the company heard it
When forming platoon "at the halt on the right"
   (Or the left, if the Captain preferred it).

And once, when the Captain was ill
   From an absence of rum in the trifle,
I gave the whole company company-drill
   Without losing a man or a rifle.

And, manfully keeping my head
    When all the battalion paraded,
I heard what the other three subalterns said,
    And I gave the same order as they did.

So, when in the Officers' Mess
    The waiter said "Cream with your coffee, Sir?"
Whatever I looked like I'm bound to confess
    That I *felt* I was really an officer.

*   *   *

I thought, when they started this war
    And asked for recruits from the many fit,
I'd rub up the knowledge I'd mastered before
    And I'd give King and Country the benefit.

The younger and fitter would fight,
    And I, being older, go slow on
The practical side of the thing, but indite
    A few notes upon marching and so on.

Alas for my knowledge! Alas
    For notes upon "dressing" and "easies"! . . .
I'll leave you to guess what a snake in the grass
    A battalion which *marches in threes* is.

The war had produced a new type—
　It seems I am quite out of touch with it;
And though it may still be correct to slope "hipe,"
　Yet I doubt if a man can do much with it.

Are privates still given C.B.?
　Or pardoned on saying they're sorry?
Field-officers booted (and spurred) to the knee—
　Do they ride on a horse or a lorry?

I find I'm no soldier at all,
　I've met, so to put it, my Munich.
Do we still clean our buttons? I cannot recall
　If we've buttons to clean on our tunic.

So now, when they talk about war,
　I sit by myself like a dumb thing
And say, when they ask "What were you in before?"
　"I was making munitions or something."

———◆———

Actually when I came to try, I found it difficult to
pose as an old soldier. I had been signalling officer in my
battalion, and had known a great deal about flags and
buzzers; but my knowledge of firearms or (as they are
called, I never discovered why) weapons of precision, was
not worth passing on. It is true that my men carried
rifles, and that I inspected them from time to time, but I

111

never knew what I was looking for. Sometimes at my request a man would open the breech and put a dirty thumb-nail at one end while I squinted down the other, and if I had seen a mouse crawling about inside I should have known that something was wrong. But I was handicapped, as I so often am, by feeling that the man was better informed than I; and that if I had said "I say, isn't that a lot of rust?" and he had said "No, sir, blood," we should have been at an impasse. I never, as they say, fired a shot in anger, and only twelve under the impetus of any other emotion. These all missed the musketry instructor, but hit the Isle of Wight. It was he who was angry.

WISHFUL THINKING

A pinch of salt (or so I've heard)
    Will make the stoutest slug go limp.
"Red" is the operative word
    Which paralyses Colonel Blimp.
A symbol with a piece of chalk
    Stops Leghorns from so much as blinking . . .
And I'm immobilised by talk
    Day in, day out, of "Wishful Thinking."

I hope tomorrow will be fine.
    I hope that no one comes to tea.
I hope this little verse of mine
    Is better than it seems to be.
And, if it is, I hope it brings
    Some golden guineas for the chinking . . .
In fact, I hope a lot of things
    Now stigmatised as Wishful Thinking.

I think our airmen simply grand.
    I think that we shall win the war—
As far as I can understand
    It's this that we are fighting for.
Our Navy is without compare,
    To all its gallant crews I'm drinking . . .
And politicians, with a stare,
    Say "Don't indulge in Wishful Thinking."

My drive (and I was dormy nine)
  Had left the green in easy reach;
The other man, by some design,
  Had put his seventh on the beach.
I watched him sliding down the cliff,
  His bag of clubs behind him clinking,
And thought that I should beat him, if—
  But that of course was Wishful Thinking.

A politician, meaning well,
  But, like a politician, fond
Of silly phrases, tripped and fell
  Head first into our village pond.
I rushed to help him with a shout,
  I bellowed, as I saw him sinking,
"Hold up, old man, I'll get you out" . . .
  "Don't! Don't!" he begged. "It's Wishful
    Thinking."
      (So I didn't.)

———◆———

If we divide England into Pundits and People, we find
that throughout this war the Pundits have been exhorting
the People against the faults which are not only most
conspicuous in themselves, but most to be reprehended in
themselves. Wishful Thinking, over-confidence, super-
optimism are not faults in the common man, they are
virtues. If his optimism led him to say: "I shan't offer my

services, because we're bound to win anyway," then it would be a fault; but his services are already at the command of the Pundits: The more hopefully and confidently he applies them, the greater their value. The danger is that the Pundit will say: "I shan't ask for his services, because we are bound to win anyway." In fact, in exhorting us not to indulge in Wishful Thinking the Pundit is really saying: "For God's sake don't be optimistic about the war. It's in my hands, and I'm utterly untrustworthy." Let us hope he is not right.

THE VOICE OF ITALY

When threats and insults filled the air,
We passed them by for what they were,
Shrugging our shoulders at the venom
Of editors who had to pen 'em.

The threats grew louder day by day . . .
We tried to look the other way.
We hoped that it was only bluff,
And hoped that Hope would be enough.

But louder still the Voice declared
The war for which it was prepared . . .
Which left us nothing else to do
But make some preparation too.

The Fleet proceeded to its station . . .
And half the Voice cried "Provocation!"
"Encircled!" screamed the other half.
I mean to say, you have to laugh.

———•—•———

But almost everything which Fascists say makes you laugh. Wells commented once on the misery which the word "Napoleonic" had brought to the world. By use of it every financial crook, every hard-faced business man, could forgive himself; for he could boast of being that admirable thing, Napoleonic. I think that greater unhappiness has been caused by the word "realistic." A "realistic attitude to the world" is an attitude which discounts all sentiment, all ideals, all art, all literature, all beauty; which, in fact, discounts all that makes life worth living. The "realist" inhabits an utterly unreal world, such as never existed; yet imagines that he alone is seeing the world as it is. If Mussolini, that arch-realist, were indeed a realist instead of an overgrown, sentimental schoolboy, he would realize the truth about Italy; which is that her contribution to civilisation always has been and always will be Beauty; not a goose-step imported from Germany, and "the song of our machine-guns."

TO AMERICA

Evil has struck again:
Again the broken faith.
And little homely lives of happiness—
The mother knitting in her rocking-chair,
The daughter, laughing, holding out proud hands
To where her baby stands
Bashful, uncertain, in its party dress—
Are twisted into fear,
Are tortured into pain,
Are closed in death.

Well, are you coming in?
It's a fight between Good and Evil,
It's a fight between God and the Devil.
Where do you stand today?
Which are you for? You have chosen, yes,
But is it enough for men to bless
The men who fight, and to turn away?
Is it enough for women to cry,
And to say "Poor things" when the innocent die?
Is it enough to give your prayers,
And then—go back to your own affairs?
It's a fight for all that you counted dear,
It's a fight for all that you fought to win;
The fight is on, and the issue clear:
Good or Evil,

God or the Devil . . .
Well, are you coming in?

Yes, "War is Hell."
But Peace is Hell if it's Peace with the Devil in power.
Yet, if this is not your quarrel and not your hour,
If you have chosen Peace, you have chosen well.
But scatter your armies, burn your ships,
Tear the breech-block out of the gun;
Never again can you fight who fight not now,
No rallying-call can ever rise to your lips,
There lives no Faith to which you can make your vow.
There is no Cause to fight for: only the one,
Only one gage of battle, only one battle-song:
Right against Wrong.

———— • ————

Perhaps by the time this appears America will be more directly engaged in the war than she is now. Meanwhile she can take comfort from this thought. The British Empire fights alone; but if Britain is submerged, and the war crosses the Atlantic, America will not fight alone. She will have Canada by her side.

THE OBJECTOR

Your Conscience is "against" the war?
So let it be. But what's it "for"?
The Peace which the Gestapo brings:
The triumph of all evil things:
Compassion, Honour, Mercy, Truth,
As practised by the Hitler Youth:
Instruction formally designed
To prostitute the infant mind,
To wean from Pastor and from Priest
Potential for a super-Beast.
Your Conscience is against the war . . .
Are these the things it's praying for?

Your Conscience thinks that War should cease;
But finds no fault with German peace,
Accepting with a careless nod
The kingdom of its anti-God.
It minds not who seduces whom
If, safe within its narrow room,
It still can hug itself and say
"We took no part in war today";
It will not mind who lost, who won,
So long as you have fired no gun.

Thus does your Conscience firmly stand
Smug in its faith, complacent, bland,
And say to Heaven "Observe me, Lord,

Your follower who drew no sword.
Then let me, from all evil freed,
For all the guilty intercede:
The wicked ones who fought to save
Your world of Beauty from the grave;
The falsely-led who overthrew
The blatant gods the heathen knew;
The ignorant who, unafraid,
Died in that ultimate Crusade.
For when I saw the Devil plain,
I said benignly 'Let him reign,'
And watched, religiously aloof,
The world beneath his cloven hoof.
And weaker men were led to fight
For what they misconceived as Right,
But I, O Lord, was not as they;
I knew Your will and turned away."

———◆———

Most of the many letters which I have had from conscientious objectors in answer to these lines have insisted
that they do not condemn the unconscientious fighter,
and do hope that we shall win the war. But, as one said in
verse:

We too would strive nor count the cost,
And know the battle can't be lost
If we but use the arms of Love,
With Hope and Courage from above . . .
The way that will not use the sword
Is that of Jesus Christ our Lord.

So, when we have won, who takes the credit? The thirty thousand who have used the arms of Love, or the three million who have used other arms? Do the thirty thousand say "There you are! I told you Love was the only way," or do they admit that, without the British Navy, Army and Air Force, Love would have left them in a concentration camp with nothing but a dehumanised sadist to practise on? In either case, since we shall all share the fruits of Victory, Freedom, the Conscientious Objector is in the position of the man who says to his family: "Although we are in danger of starvation, my conscience does not allow me to steal. But I do not reproach you for stealing, since your conscience does allow you to. So I hope you will be thoroughly successful in your efforts tonight, and then we can all have a good meal."

Finally, I think that there is a difference between refusing to "use the sword" to defend oneself, and refusing to use it to defend the innocent and helpless. I cannot believe that, if Christ in His journeys had come across a sadist torturing a child, He would have been content to preach a parable. The Conscientious Objector does believe this.

THE LOST GENERATION

You were the Lost Generation, decadent, nerveless,
    slack
  (Born to the sound of the guns and of death drop-
    ping down from the air)
You slouched to your casual dates with a languorous
    curve to your back,
  And we didn't admire your manners, and loathed
    the length of your hair.

We stood in front of the fireplace and eased our
    stiffening hocks
  (We who had fought in Flanders, we who had
    flown in France)
And damned the whole generation—you and your
    girlish locks!—
  Poor effeminate creatures, boys who had had no
    chance.

We pitied you more than blamed you; what could you
    hope to be,
  Born to the fear of war by frightened women, and
    then
Living your life with women whose men were over
    the sea?
  Taught to be men by women—how could you grow
    to be men?

Youth of the Lost Generation, sons of the men that
  were,
  Taught to be men by women who made you all that
    you are,
How could you grow to be men, who have grown to
    be gods of the Air,
  Who have set in the skies for our nerving a flame of
    Faith like a star?

Each night we crouch by the fireplace, and listen with
    tight-held breath,
  Humbled to tears in wonder, strengthened to tears
    in pride,
As the Youth which we dared to pity makes casual
    date with Death,
  And, fired by a spirit we know not, goes off on its
    deathless ride.

———•———

With which salute to brave men I close. It is June
now; one of those lovely, still, country evenings, blue and
green and golden; such an evening as almost compels
faith in the doubting, courage in the fearful, by the calm
assurance of its beauty. Italy is in the war. France has
fallen. Well, we are alone. Much will have happened before these words are in print, but, be it good or ill, may
we live and die as gallantly, as those happy few, upheld
by something of their spirit.

———•———